Cottages
IN CROSS STITCH

Gail Bussi

MEREHURST

THE CHARTS
Some of the designs in this book are very detailed and due to
inevitable space limitations, the charts may be shown on a
comparatively small scale; in such cases, readers may find it
helpful to have the particular chart with which they are
currently working enlarged.

THREADS
The projects in this book were all stitched with DMC stranded cotton
embroidery threads. The keys given with each chart also list thread
combinations for those who wish to use Anchor or Madeira threads.
It should be pointed out that the shades produced by different
companies vary slightly, and it is not always possible to find
identical colours in a different range.

Published in 1994 by Merehurst Limited
Ferry House, 51-57 Lacy Road, Putney, London SW15 1PR

Reprinted 1996

Text © Copyright 1994 Gail Bussi
Photography & illustrations © Copyright 1994 Merehurst Limited
ISBN 1 85391 397 9

A catalogue record for this book is available from the British Library.

Managing Editor Heather Dewhurst
Edited by Diana Lodge
Designed by Maggie Aldred
Photography by Marie-Louise Avery
Illustrations by John Hutchinson
Typesetting by BMD Graphics, Hemel Hempstead
Colour separation by Fotographics Limited, UK – Hong Kong
Printed in Hong Kong by Wing King Tong

*Merehurst is the leading publisher of craft books and has an excellent range
of titles to suit all levels. Please send to the address above for our
free catalogue, stating the title of this book.*

CONTENTS

$\mathcal{I}$NTRODUCTION

Cross stitch – the traditional art of counting stitches – is enjoying a tremendous revival in popularity, and justifiably so, for with only a few basic skills and stitches, anyone from the novice to the experienced needleworker can create an almost limitless range of designs.

The English cottage – charming, traditional and immensely varied in its style and appearance – remains the archetypal image of what we all imagine as the idealized country dwelling: peaceful, quaint and unchanging. Somehow, cottages seem particularly suited to designs in the cross stitch medium, lending themselves very well to the colours and effects available.

In this book you will find a wide range of cottage designs, to suit all tastes and levels of ability; there are cottages in seasonal settings, traditional cottages, and tiny cottages that are ideal when you want something quick to stitch. Many of the cottages are stitched as pictures that would be a lovely addition to any home – city or country – but there are also pillows and other gifts, taking cottage designs as their theme. All in all, there is a feast of stitching ideas here for all needleworkers who love the gentle peace of these charming homes.

$\mathcal{B}$ASIC SKILLS

BEFORE YOU BEGIN

PREPARING THE FABRIC

Even with an average amount of handling, many evenweave fabrics tend to fray at the edges, so it is a good idea to overcast the raw edges, using ordinary sewing thread, before you begin.

FABRIC

All projects in this book use Aida fabric, which is ideal both for beginners and more advanced stitchers as it has a surface of clearly designated squares. All Aida fabric has a count, which refers to the number of squares (each stitch covers one square) to one inch (2.5cm); the higher the count, the smaller the finished stitching. Projects in this book use either 14- or 18-count Aida, two popular and readily available sizes, in a wide variety of colours.

THE INSTRUCTIONS

Each project begins with a full list of the materials that you will require. The measurements given for the embroidery fabric include a minimum of 5cm (2in) all around to allow for stretching it in a frame and preparing the edges to prevent them from fraying.

Colour keys for stranded embroidery cottons – DMC, Anchor or Madeira – are given with each chart. It is assumed that you will need to buy one skein of each colour mentioned in a particular key, even though you may use less, but where two or more skeins are needed, this information is included in the main list of requirements.

To work from the charts, particularly those where several symbols are used in close proximity, some readers may find it helpful to have the chart enlarged so that the squares and symbols can be seen more easily. Many photocopying services will do this for a minimum charge.

Before you begin to embroider, always mark the centre of the design with two lines of basting stitches, one vertical and one horizontal, running from edge to edge of the fabric, as indicated by the arrows on the charts.

As you stitch, use the centre lines given on the chart and the basting threads on your fabric as reference points for counting the squares and threads to position your design accurately.

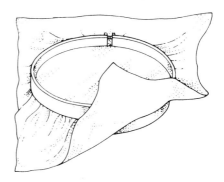

WORKING IN A RECTANGULAR FRAME

Rectangular frames are more suitable for larger pieces of embroidery. They consist of two rollers, with tapes attached, and two flat side pieces, which slot into the rollers and are held in place by pegs or screw attachments. Available in different sizes, either alone or with adjustable table or floor stands, frames are measured by the length of the roller tape, and range in size from 30cm (12in) to 68cm (27in).

As alternatives to a slate frame, canvas stretchers and the backs of old picture frames can be used. Provided there is sufficient extra fabric around the finished size of the embroidery, the edges can be turned under and simply attached with drawing pins (thumb tacks) or staples.

WORKING IN A HOOP

A hoop is the most popular frame for use with small areas of embroidery. It consists of two rings, one fitted inside the other; the outer ring usually has an adjustable screw attachment so that it can be tightened to hold the stretched fabric in place. Hoops are available in several sizes, ranging from 10cm (4in) in diameter to quilting hoops with a diameter of 38cm (15in). Hoops with table stands or floor stands attached are also available.

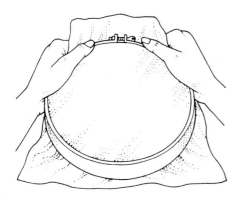

1 To stretch your fabric in a hoop, place the area to be embroidered over the inner ring and press the outer ring over it, with the tension screw released. Tissue paper can be placed between the outer ring and the embroidery, so that the hoop does not mark the fabric. Lay the tissue paper over the fabric when you set it in the hoop, then tear away the central embroidery area.

2 Smooth the fabric and, if necessary, straighten the grain before tightening the screw. The fabric should be evenly stretched.

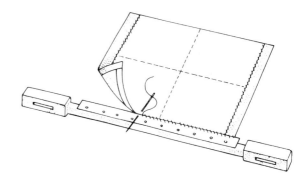

1 To stretch your fabric in a rectangular frame, cut out the fabric, allowing at least an extra 5cm (2in) all around the finished size of the embroidery. Baste a single 12mm (½in) turning on the top and bottom edges and oversew strong tape, 2.5cm (1in) wide, to the other two sides. Mark the centre line both ways with basting stitches. Working from the centre outward and using strong thread, oversew the top

5

and bottom edges to the roller tapes. Fit the side pieces into the slots, and roll any extra fabric on one roller until the fabric is taut.

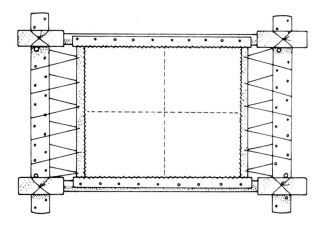

2 Insert the pegs or adjust the screw attachments to secure the frame. Thread a large-eyed needle (chenille needle) with strong thread or fine string and lace both edges, securing the ends around the intersections of the frame. Lace the webbing at 2.5cm (1in) intervals, stretching the fabric evenly.

EXTENDING EMBROIDERY FABRIC

It is easy to extend a piece of embroidery fabric, such as a bookmark, to stretch it in a hoop.

● Fabric oddments of a similar weight can be used. Simply cut four pieces to size (in other words, to the measurement that will fit both the embroidery fabric and your hoop) and baste them to each side of the embroidery fabric before stretching it in the hoop in the usual way.

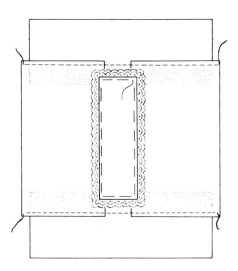

MOUNTING EMBROIDERY

The cardboard should be cut to the size of the finished embroidery, with an extra 6mm (¼in) added all round to allow for the recess in the frame.

LIGHTWEIGHT FABRICS

1 Place embroidery face down, with the cardboard centred on top, and basting and pencil lines matching. Begin by folding over the fabric at each corner and securing it with masking tape.

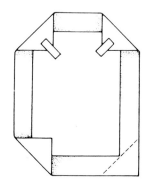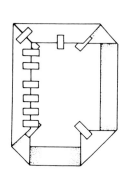

2 Working first on one side and then the other, fold over the fabric on all sides and secure it firmly with pieces of masking tape, placed about 2.5cm (1in) apart. Also neaten the mitred corners with masking tape, pulling the fabric tightly to give a firm, smooth finish.

HEAVIER FABRICS

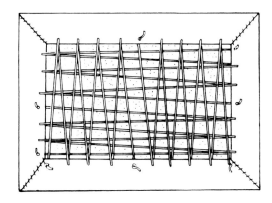

● Lay the embroidery face down, with the cardboard centred on top; fold over the edges of the fabric on opposite sides, making mitred folds at the corners, and lace across, using strong thread. Repeat on the other two sides. Finally, pull up the fabric firmly over the cardboard. Overstitch the mitred corners.

CROSS STITCH

For all cross stitch embroidery, the following two methods of working are used. In each case, neat rows of vertical stitches are produced on the back of the fabric.

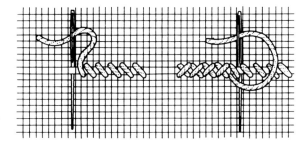

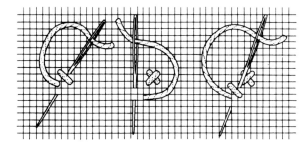

● When stitching large areas, work in horizontal rows. Working from right to left, complete the first row of evenly spaced diagonal stitches over the number of threads specified in the project instructions. Then, working from left to right, repeat the process. Continue in this way, making sure each stitch crosses in the same direction.

● When stitching diagonal lines, work downwards, completing each stitch before moving to the next. When starting a project always begin to embroider at the centre of the design and work outwards to ensure that the design will be placed centrally on the fabric.

BACKSTITCH

Backstitch is used in the projects to give emphasis to a particular foldline, an outline or a shadow. The stitches are worked over the same number of threads as the cross stitch, forming continuous straight or diagonal lines.

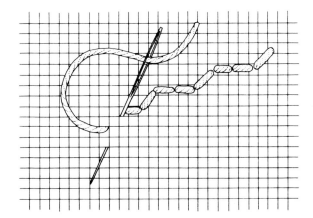

● Make the first stitch from left to right; pass the needle behind the fabric and bring it out one stitch length ahead to the left. Repeat and continue in this way along the line.

QUARTER CROSS STITCHES

Some fractional stitches are used on certain projects in this book; although they strike fear into the hearts of less experienced stitchers they are not difficult to master, and give a more natural line in certain instances. Should you find it difficult to pierce the centre of the Aida block, simply use a sharp needle to make a small hole in the centre first.

To work a quarter cross, bring the needle up at point A and down through the centre of the square at B. Later, the diagonal back stitch finishes the stitch. A chart square with two different symbols separated by a diagonal line requires two quarter stitches. Backstitch will later finish the square.

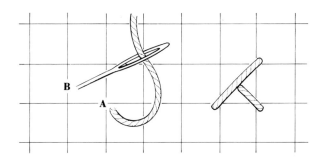

Spring Cottage

A half-timbered cottage stands under a canopy of blossom in a spring landscape that echoes the freshness of the season. This is the first of four seasonal pictures, and will bring a touch of spring to any home.

SPRING COTTAGE

YOU WILL NEED

For the Spring Cottage picture, set in a mount with a cut-out measuring 16.5cm × 21.5cm (6½in × 8½in):

30cm × 35cm (12in × 14in) of antique white, 14-count Aida fabric
Stranded embroidery cotton in the colours given in the panel
No 26 tapestry needle
Wooden frame, measuring 26cm × 30cm (10⅜in × 12in)
Rectangular mount, cut to fit the frame, with cut-out as specified above
Strong thread and cardboard, for mounting

•

THE EMBROIDERY

Prepare the fabric as described on page 4; find the centre by folding, and mark the horizontal and vertical centre lines with basting stitches in a light-coloured thread. Set the fabric in a frame or hoop and count out from the centre to start stitching at a point convenient to you.

Two threads of cotton were used in the needle for cross stitches and one for backstitch, *unless* otherwise stated on the colour key. Work all full cross stitches first, and then the half crosses, taking them over one block of fabric. Make sure that all top stitches run in the same direction. Finally, work all backstitch details.

FINISHING

Gently handwash the finished piece, if necessary, and lightly press with a steam iron on the wrong side. Finally, stretch and mount the embroidery as explained on page 6. Insert it into the frame, behind the rectangular mount. A subtle wooden frame has been used for all four seasonal cottage pictures, and the colour of the mount has been especially selected in each case to echo colours predominant in the design.

Cross	Half Cross		DMC	ANCHOR	MADEIRA
		SPRING COTTAGE ▶			
⊞		White	White	2	White
○		Medium olive green	3053	859	1510
▲		Dark beige grey	640	903	1905
∨		Medium beige grey	642	392	1906
⊡		Light beige grey	644	830	1907
◉		Dark olive green	3052	844	1509
◪		Dark brown	839	360	1914
⊘		Medium salmon pink	760	9	0405
∧		Light salmon pink	761	8	0404
■		Dark grey	844	401	1810
T		Golden tan	420	375	2104
●		Light blue grey	927	849	1708
◤	⧄	Medium grey green	522	859	1513
·	▫	Very light grey green	524	858	1511
L		Light yellow	744	301	0112
Y		Very light yellow	745	300	0111
	◣	Light tan	437	362	2012
	⊏	Very light tan	738	942	2013
◇		Apple green	368	261	1310
●		Clear green	3363	262	1311
⊔		Light clear green	3364	843	1603
⊟		Beige	3033	387	2001
	N	Very soft blue	3753	158	1014
✕		Golden brown	612	832	2108
		Dark golden brown*	611	898	2107

Note: bks roof, house, door and birds with one strand only of dark golden brown (used for bks only) in the needle, and window panes with two strands of white; when using very soft blue, stitch with one strand only; very light green is used for cross stitches in the background and half cross stitches in the foreground; very light tan, apple green, and very soft blue are used for half cross stitches only.*

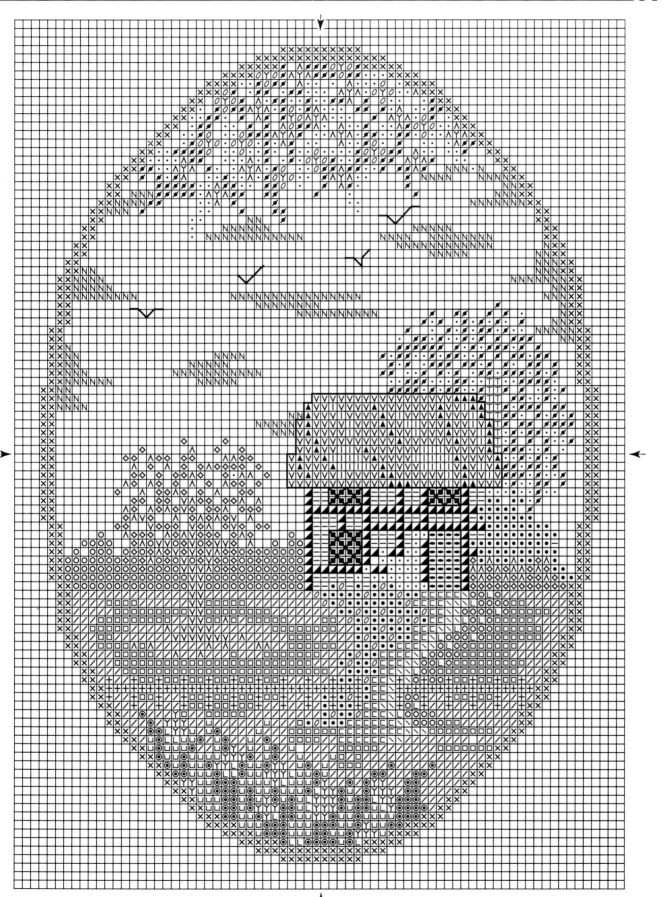

Traditional Cottages

The English cottage is known all over
the world as exemplifying the cottage
at its most charming and traditional.
In these designs, three different
cottages have been stitched to create
a set of delightful small pictures.

TRADITIONAL COTTAGES

YOU WILL NEED

For each Traditional Cottage picture, set in a rectangular frame, measuring 15cm × 12.5cm (6in × 5in):

22.5cm × 20cm (9in × 8in) of antique white, 18-count Aida fabric
Stranded embroidery cotton in the colours given in the appropriate panel
No 26 tapestry needle
Wooden frame, as specified above
Strong thread and cardboard, for mounting

NOTE: these designs have been stitched as miniatures; should you prefer larger pictures, simply use linen with a coarser weave, and two strands of embroidery cotton. Several shades of cotton have been used in all three pictures. If you are making the set, you will only require one skein of each colour.

•

THE EMBROIDERY

Prepare the fabric as described on page 4; find the centre by folding, and mark the horizontal and vertical centre lines with basting stitches in a light-coloured thread. Set the fabric in a hoop or frame, and count out from the centre to start stitching at a point convenient to you.

One thread of cotton was used in the needle for cross stitches and one for backstitch throughout these designs. Work all cross stitches first, making sure that all top stitches run in the same direction. Finally, work all backstitch details. When stitching The Lodge, the effect of diamond window panes is made by taking long diagonal stitches across each window pane, using one strand of cotton. Use the photograph as a guide when making these stitches.

FINISHING

Gently handwash the finished piece, if necessary, and lightly press with a steam iron on the wrong side. Stretch and mount the embroidery as explained on page 6. Insert it into the frame. Simple wooden frames were used with each of these pictures to avoid overwhelming the design.

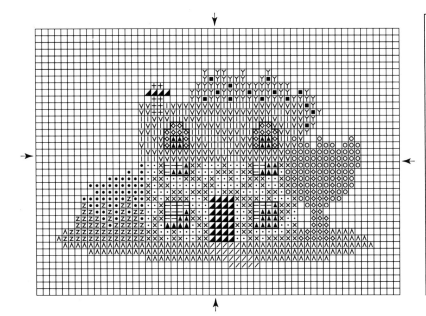

BROADWAY COTTAGE ◄			DMC	ANCHOR	MADEIRA
Cross	Half Cross				
◢		Red brown	433	371	2303
▲		Dark steel grey	414	235	1801
⊟		Medium steel grey	318	399	1802
⊠		Medium straw	3046	887	2206
·		Light straw	3047	886	2205
▪		Light salmon pink	761	8	0404
○	∧	Light olive green	3053	860	1605
●		Clear green	3363	262	1311
Z		Light grey green	523	859	1509
Y		Very light grey green	524	858	1511
◇		Medium golden brown	611	898	2107
+		Dark golden brown	610	905	1914
V		Medium grey brown	642	392	1906
I		Light grey brown	644	830	1907
	⁄	Tan	437	362	2012
		White*	White	2	White
		Very dark grey*	844	401	1810

Note: bks window panes with white* and dormers, window frames and door with very dark grey* (both used for bks only).

THE LODGE ▶			DMC	ANCHOR	MADEIRA
Cross	Half Cross				
▲		Medium golden brown	611	898	2107
Z		Clear green	3363	262	1311
∧		Khaki	3013	854	1605
●		Red brown	433	371	2303
V		Medium golden tan	420	889	2010
·		Ecru	Ecru	926	2101
✕		Pale beige	3033	392	1903
◇		Medium grey brown	642	399	1906
—		Light grey brown	644	830	1907
■		Light sallmon pink	761	8	0404
Y		Yellow	744	301	0112
I		Dark steel grey	414	400	1801
⚡		Apple green	368	261	1310
⟍		Light grey green	523	859	1509
O	∕	Light olive green	3053	860	1605
	+	Tan	437	362	2012
		Dark grey*	844	401	1810
		White*	White	2	White

Note: bks window frames and door in very dark grey, and window panes in white* (both used for bks only).*

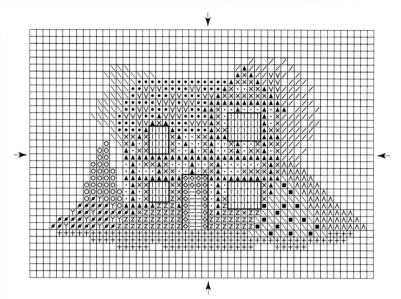

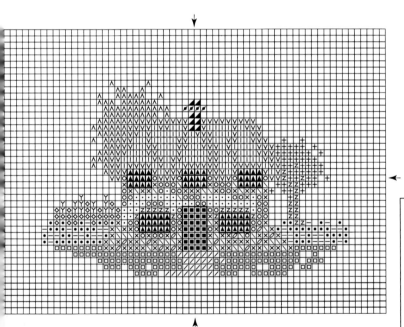

BADGER'S COTTAGE ◀			DMC	ANCHOR	MADEIRA
Cross	Half Cross				
◤		Dark golden brown	610	905	1914
⚡		Medium golden tan	420	889	2010
V		Medium straw	3046	887	2206
I		Light straw	3047	886	2205
▲		Dark grey	645	400	1811
·		White	White	2	White
O		Light silver grey	762	397	1804
■		Medium pink brown	3064	378	2310
Z		Medium golden brown	611	898	2107
✕		Light olive green	3053	860	1605
⊘		Light salmon pink	760	9	0405
⟍		Very light grey green	524	858	1511
	∕	Tan	437	368	2012
●		Medium grey brown	642	392	1906
—		Light grey brown	644	830	1907
	∧	Light grey green	523	859	1512
+	⊡	Clear green	3363	262	1311
◇		Apple green	368	261	1310
Y		Light blue	3752	976	1710
		Very dark grey*	844	401	1810

Note: bks window frames and door in very dark grey (used for bks only), and window panes in white.*

'In a Cottage Garden' Pillow

This design is reminiscent of
traditional sampler styles, with its
rows of stylized flowers and leaves,
but it has been interpreted in the style
of the typical English cottage garden
and made up as a small pillow.
To carry the garden theme still further
you could insert a small amount of
scented potpourri into the pillow.

'IN A COTTAGE GARDEN'

YOU WILL NEED

For the pillow, measuring 23cm (9in) square, excluding the lace trim:

30cm (12in) square of white, 18-count Aida fabric
Stranded embroidery cotton in the colours given in the panel
No 26 tapestry needle
1.1m (1⅓yds) of gathered broderie anglaise, 3cm (1¼in) wide
25cm (10in) square of backing fabric
4 white ribbon roses
Polyester filling
Pot pourri (optional)

●

THE EMBROIDERY

Prepare the fabric as described on page 4; find the centre by folding, and mark the horizontal and vertical centre lines with basting stitches in a light-coloured thread. Set the fabric in a frame or hoop, and count out from the centre to start stitching at a point convenient to you.

One thread of cotton was used in the needle for cross stitches and for backstitch throughout the design. Work all cross stitches first, making sure that all top stitches run in the same direction. Finally, work all backstitch details.

MAKING THE PILLOW

Gently handwash the finished piece, if necessary, and lightly press with a steam iron on the wrong side. Trim the embroidered fabric to measure 25cm (10in) square. Pin the broderie anglaise to the right side of the embroidery, with the decorative edge facing inwards. Trim the ends, if necessary, and join them with a neat french seam.

Gathering it slightly at the corners, baste the broderie anglaise in place, lying just inside the 12mm (½in) seam allowance. With right sides together, pin and stitch the backing fabric and embroidered piece together, leaving a gap of 5cm (2in) at one side.

Clip the corners; turn the cover right side out, and fill with polyester, adding the pot pourri if this is to be included. Slipstitch the opening, and finish by stitching a ribbon rose in each corner of the cushion.

IN A COTTAGE GARDEN ▶		DMC	ANCHOR	MADEIRA
◇	Medium grey green	522	860	1513
O	Light grey green	523	859	1512
·	Very light grey green	524	858	1511
▲	Medium golden brown	611	898	2107
⊟	Golden brown	612	832	2108
▨	Medium antique violet	3041	870	0806
▣	Light antique violet	3042	869	0807
⊡	Pale cream	822	390	1908
⋀	Medium beige grey	642	853	1906
⧄	Light beige grey	644	830	1907
◣	Sky blue	3752	976	1001
◎	Silver grey	415	398	1803
Y	Yellow	744	301	0112
V	Apple green	368	261	1310
●	Clear green	3363	262	1311
✛	Light clear green	3364	266	1501
Z	Medium salmon pink	760	9	0405
X	Light salmon pink	761	8	0404
╱	Light shell pink	3713	48	0502
■	Dark grey	3022	392	1903
	White*	White	2	White

Note: bks house walls, door, roof and outer windows in dark grey; use clear green for inner and outer border, and white* (used for bks only) for window panes.

Summer Cottage

This picture offers what has to be the quintessential image of an English summer scene – the golden thatched cottage covered with creepers and climbing roses and surrounded by the typical English cottage garden, a riot of scent and colour.

SUMMER COTTAGE

YOU WILL NEED

For the Summer Cottage picture, set in a mount with a cut-out measuring 16.5cm × 21.5cm (6½in × 8½in):

30cm × 35cm (12in × 14in) of antique white, 14-count Aida fabric
Stranded embroidery cotton in the colours given in the panel
No 26 tapestry needle
Wooden frame, measuring 26cm × 30cm (10⅜in × 12in)
Rectangular mount, cut to fit the frame, with cut-out as specified above
Strong thread and cardboard, for mounting

•

THE EMBROIDERY

Prepare the fabric as described on page 4; find the centre by folding, and mark the horizontal and vertical centre lines with basting stitches in a light-coloured thread. Set the fabric in a frame or hoop, and count out from the centre to start stitching at a point convenient to you.

Two threads of cotton were used in the needle for cross stitches and one for backstitch, *unless otherwise stated on the colour key*. Work all full cross stitches first, and then the half crosses, taking them over one block of fabric. Make sure that all top stitches run in the same direction. Finally, work all backstitch details.

FINISHING

Gently handwash the finished piece, if necessary, and lightly press with a steam iron on the wrong side. Stretch and mount the embroidery as explained on page 6. Insert it into the frame, behind the rectangular mount. A subtle wooden frame has been used for all four seasonal cottage pictures, and the colour of the mount has been especially selected in each case to echo colours predominant in the design.

SUMMER COTTAGE ▶			DMC	ANCHOR	MADEIRA
Cross	Half Cross				
☒		Golden brown	612	832	2108
◪		Dark golden brown	611	898	2107
◯		Soft apple green	368	261	1310
●		Clear green	3363	262	1311
Ⓛ	◲	Medium grey green	522	859	1513
◩		Medium straw	3047	887	2206
Ⅰ		Light straw	3046	886	2205
■		Very dark grey	844	401	1810
Y		Yellow	744	301	0112
+		Soft antique mauve	3042	869	0807
▲		Medium salmon pink	760	9	0405
◖		Light salmon pink	761	8	0404
—		Soft shell pink	3713	48	0502
Ⓒ		Soft clear green	3364	266	1501
∧		Very light grey green	524	858	1511
╱		White	White	2	White
⊘		Pale cream	822	390	1908
Ⓩ		Medium olive green	3053	844	1510
◉		Medium grey blue	926	779	1707
Ⓣ		Light grey blue	927	849	1708
Ⅱ		Very light grey blue	928	900	1709
	⊡	Light beige grey	644	830	1907
	⊻	Medium beige grey	642	392	1906
	◈	Pale blue	3752	9159	1002

Note: bks roof, house, door and window surrounds with one strand only of medium golden brown in the needle, and window panes with two strands of white; use one strand only when making half cross stitches with pale blue.

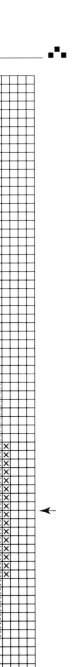

Traditional Cottage Sampler

The traditional sampler with its
border, floral motifs and alphabet has
enjoyed a tremendous revival in
popularity in recent years.
This sampler is a fresh approach to
the theme featuring delicate colours,
a heartwarming quotation and a
vignette of a thatched cottage set
in a pretty garden.

TRADITIONAL COTTAGE SAMPLER

YOU WILL NEED

For the Traditional Cottage sampler, set in a frame measuring 20cm × 25cm (8in × 10in):

25cm × 30cm (10in × 12in) of antique white, 18-count Aida fabric
Stranded embroidery cotton in the colours given in the panel
No 26 tapestry needle
Wooden frame, as specified above
Strong thread and cardboard, for mounting

●

THE EMBROIDERY

Prepare the fabric as described on page 4; find the centre by folding, and mark the horizontal and vertical centre lines with basting stitches in a light-coloured thread. Set the fabric in a frame, and count out from the centre to start stitching at a point convenient to you.

One thread of cotton was used in the needle for cross stitches and one for backstitch throughout this design. Work all cross stitches first, and then the half crosses, taking them over one block of fabric. Make sure that all top stitches run in the same direction. (Please note that some quarter stitches are used in this design – an explanation of how to do these stitches is given on page 7.) Finally, work all backstitch details.

FINISHING

Gently handwash the finished piece, if necessary, and lightly press with a steam iron on the wrong side. Stretch and mount the embroidery as explained on page 6. Insert it into the frame. A fairly traditional style of wooden frame looks most suitable with this type of design.

TRADITIONAL COTTAGE ▶			DMC	ANCHOR	MADEIRA
Cross	Half Cross				
●		Silver grey	415	398	1803
		Dark grey blue*	926	779	1707
✕		Light grey blue	927	849	1708
⊂		Very light grey blue	928	900	1709
Z		Light shell pink	3713	48	0502
N		Light salmon pink	761	8	0404
▲		Medium salmon pink	760	9	0405
◖		Clear green	3363	262	1311
O		Medium grey green	522	859	1513
L	・	Light grey green	524	858	1511
◉		Soft antique violet	3042	869	0807
─	◣	Apple green	368	261	1310
◢		Medium golden brown	611	898	2107
⊔		Light tan	437	362	2012
✚		Dark brown	839	360	1914
◈		Olive green	3053	844	1510
I		Very light beige	3033	387	2001
V		Beige	3782	388	1906
⁄		Light steel grey	648	900	1814
Y		Medium steel grey	647	8581	1813
■		Very dark steel grey	645	400	1811

Note: bks inner and outer border and lettering in dark grey blue (used for bks only), hearts in medium salmon pink, flourishes with hearts in medium grey green, window panes in white* (used for bks only) and roof, chimneys and door in medium golden brown.*

HOME IS WHERE THE HEART IS

Little Houses

Small motifs of cottages make delightful pictures, trinkets, gifts and cards – suitable for many occasions. They also make an ideal starting point for the newcomer to cross stitch as they are quick and easy to stitch. Five separate designs are given here, each made up in a different format.

LITTLE HOUSES

YOU WILL NEED

For each design you will require the following:

13cm (5¼in) square of linen (see individual item
for the thread count)
Stranded embroidery cotton in the colours given in
the appropriate panel
No 26 tapestry needle

For the Gift Tag, measuring 5cm (2in) square:

Antique white, 18-count Aida fabric
Gift tag (for suppliers, see page 48)

For the Key Ring, measuring 4cm (1½in)
in diameter:

Antique white, 18-count Aida fabric
Key ring (for suppliers, see page 48)

For the Oval Box, with a lid measuring
approximately 7cm × 5cm (2¾in × 2in):

Antique white, 18-count Aida fabric
Soft pink porcelain box (for suppliers see page 48)

For the Round Box, measuring approximately
6.5cm (2½in) in diameter:

Antique white, 14-count Aida fabric
Round ivory porcelain box (for suppliers,
see page 48)

For the Card, measuring 10cm × 6.5cm
(4in × 2½in), with an oval opening:

Antique white, 14-count Aida fabric
Purchased card (for suppliers, see page 48)

•

THE EMBROIDERY

Each design uses only a small amount of fabric, which makes these projects an ideal way of using up off-cuts. On the other hand, if you have no odd pieces of fabric, you may prefer to embroider designs in batches – gift tag, key ring and oval box, or round box and card – to avoid waste.

For each design, prepare the fabric as described on page 4, and mark the horizontal and vertical centre lines with basting stitches in a light-coloured thread. Set the fabric in a hoop and count out from the centre to start stitching at a point convenient to you. Work all cross stitches first, making sure that all top stitches run in the same direction. Finally, work all backstitch details.

For the gift tag, key ring and oval porcelain box, use one strand of embroidery cotton in the needle when making cross stitches and also for back-stitching. For the round porcelain box and card, use two strands of thread in the needle when making the cross stitches, and one for backstitching.

Gently handwash the finished piece, if necessary, and lightly press with a steam iron on the wrong side. Follow the manufacturer's instructions for assembly.

OVAL BOX ▼			DMC	ANCHOR	MADEIRA
Cross	Half Cross				
▼		Apple green	368	261	1310
⊘		Soft blue	3752	343	1001
▢		Light salmon pink	761	8	0404
•		White	White	2	White
z		Light golden brown	612	832	2108
◣		Medium steel grey	646	815	1811
×		Medium straw	3046	373	2103
C		Light straw	3047	886	2205
◪		Medium grey green	522	860	1602
+		Medium pink brown	3064	378	2310
◁		Ecru	Ecru	926	2101
	◩	Tan	437	368	2011
⓪		Very light grey green	524	858	1511
		Medium golden brown*	611	898	2107

Note: bks around window frames and panes with white, and around window frames, door and fence with medium golden brown (used for bks only).*

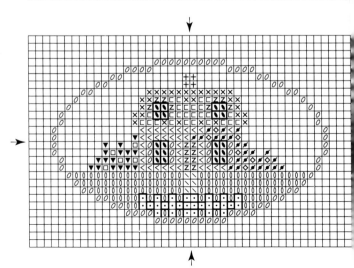

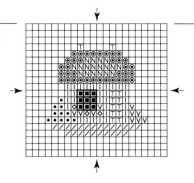

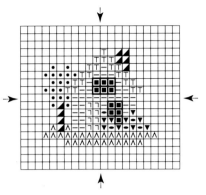

GIFT TAG ▲

Cross Half Cross

			DMC	ANCHOR	MADEIRA
◉		Medium grey beige	3022	8581	1903
N		Light grey beige	3023	392	1902
T		Medium golden tan	420	889	2010
■		Dark steel grey	645	400	1811
•		Clear green	3363	262	1311
◇		Medium salmon pink	760	9	0405
V		Light grey green	523	859	1512
I		Beige	3033	392	1903
	⁄	Very light gold brown	613	831	2109
		White*	White	2	White

Note: bks window panes with one strand of white* (used for bks only).

KEY RING ▲

Cross Half Cross

			DMC	ANCHOR	MADEIRA
T		Medium golden tan	420	889	2010
■		Dark steel grey	645	400	1811
•		Clear green	3363	262	1311
▲		Medium golden brown	611	898	2107
˥		Red brown	433	371	2303
▼		Apple green	368	261	1310
◐		Medium antique blue	932	920	1710
−		Soft pink brown	3773	882	2312
	∧	Light grey green	523	859	1512
		White*	White	2	White

Note: bks window frames and panes with one strand of white* (used for bks only).

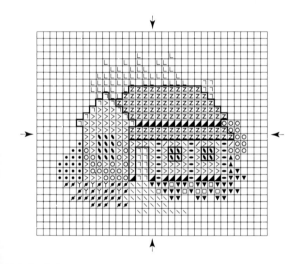

ROUND BOX ▲

Cross Half Cross

			DMC	ANCHOR	MADEIRA
•		Clear green	3363	262	1311
◣		Medium golden brown	611	898	2107
˥		Red brown	433	371	2303
▼		Apple green	368	261	1310
◐		Medium antique blue	932	920	1710
◻		Light salmon pink	761	8	0404
Z		Light golden brown	612	832	2108
◪		Medium steel grey	646	815	1811
◤		Medium grey green	522	860	1602
	◥	Tan	437	368	2011
	L	Very light grey green	524	858	1511
O		Light olive green	3053	216	1513
Y		Yellow	744	301	0112
>		Light silver grey	762	397	1804
▲		Dark golden brown	610	905	1914
		White*	White	2	White

Note: bks with white* (used for bks only) around window frames and panes, and dark golden brown for walls and roof.

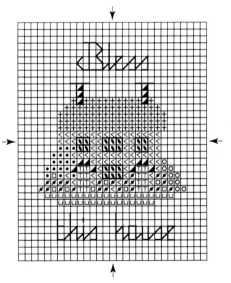

CARD ▲

Cross Half Cross

			DMC	ANCHOR	MADEIRA
T		Medium golden tan	420	889	2010
•		Clear green	3363	262	1311
◣		Medium golden brown	611	898	2107
	⊔	Apple green	368	261	1310
◻		Light salmon pink	761	8	0404
◪		Medium steel grey	646	815	1811
◎		Light olive green	3053	216	1513
		White*	White	2	White
		Dark steel grey*	645	400	1811
		Dark golden brown*	610	905	1914

Note: bks with white* for window panes, dark steel grey* for lettering, and dark golden brown* (all used for bks only) for window frames and chimneys.

Autumn
Cottage

'Season of mists and mellow
fruitfulness' – the autumn of John
Keats is also a time of ripening and
harvest, golden fruit and falling
leaves and, everywhere, rich
autumnal colours. Here a brick
cottage nestles behind an old grey
stone wall, close to the splendour of
a tree in all its autumn foliage.

AUTUMN COTTAGE

YOU WILL NEED

For the Autumn Cottage picture, set in a mount with a cut-out measuring 16.5cm × 21.5cm (6½in × 8½in):

30cm × 35cm (12in × 14in) of antique white, 14-count Aida fabric
Stranded embroidery cotton in the colours given in the panel
No 26 tapestry needle
Wooden frame, measuring 26cm × 30cm (10⅜in × 12in)
Rectangular mount, cut to fit the frame, with a cut-out as specified above
Strong thread and cardboard, for mounting

•

THE EMBROIDERY

Prepare the fabric as described on page 4; find the centre by folding, and mark the horizontal and vertical centre lines with basting stitches in a light-coloured thread. Set the fabric in a frame or hoop and count out from the centre to start stitching at a point convenient to you.

Two threads of cotton were used in the needle for cross stitches and one for backstitch *unless* otherwise stated on the colour key. Work all full cross stitches first, and then the half crosses, taking them over one block of fabric. Make sure that all top stitches run in the same direction. Finally, work all backstitch details.

FINISHING

Gently handwash the finished piece, if necessary, and lightly press with a steam iron on the wrong side. Finally, stretch and mount the embroidery as explained on page 6. Insert it into the frame, behind the rectangular mount. A subtle wooden frame has been used for all seasonal cottage pictures, and the colour of the mount has been especially selected in each case to echo colours predominant in the design.

AUTUMN COTTAGE ▶			DMC	ANCHOR	MADEIRA
Cross	Half Cross				
X		Golden brown	612	832	2108
▲		Medium steel grey	647	8581	1813
I		Light steel grey	648	900	1814
O		Clear green	3363	262	1311
◢		Medium golden brown	611	898	2107
●		Dark peach	351	10	0214
◇		Medium peach	352	9	0303
Y		Yellow	744	301	0112
■		Very dark grey	844	401	1810
V	◨	Light golden brown	613	831	2109
T		Light tan	437	362	2012
▭		Very light tan	738	942	2013
◪	◿	Dusky peach	3773	883	2312
C		Soft peach	754	6	0305
	⊡	Soft clear green	3364	843	1603
	N	Very light grey blue	928	900	1709
Z		Tan †	420	375	2104
		Dark straw †	3045	888	2103
		†Combine one strand of each			
		White*	White	2	White

Note: bks roof, leaves, door and apples with one strand only of medium golden brown in the needle, and window panes with two strands of white* (used for bks only).

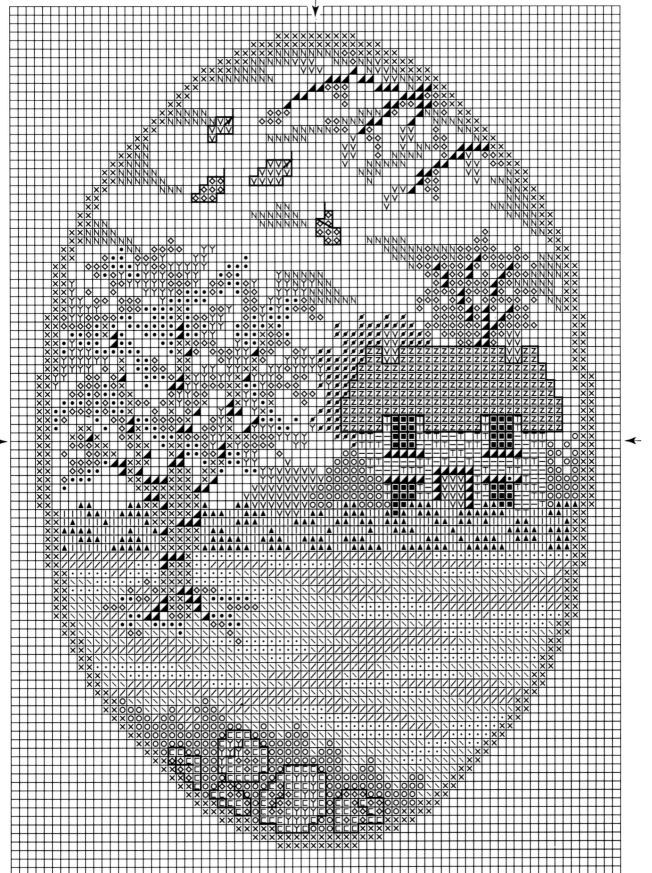

Baby Birth Pillow

The birth of a baby is always something to celebrate, and what better way to remember this special event could there be than by stitching this personalized pillow in delicate shades, featuring a gingerbread cottage straight out of a fairytale? It would make a treasured gift for any new mother or grandmother; if preferred, it could also be stitched as a small picture.

BABY BIRTH PILLOW

YOU WILL NEED

For the Gingerbread Cottage birth pillow, measuring 21cm (8½in) square, excluding the trim:

30cm (12in) square of white, 18-count Aida fabric
Stranded embroidery cotton in the colours given in the panel
No26 tapestry needle
1.2m (1⅓yds) of gathered broderie anglais, 2cm (¾in) wide
23cm (9¼in) square of backing fabric
4 pink ribbon bows
Polyester filling

•

THE EMBROIDERY

Prepare the fabric as described on page 4; find the centre by folding, and mark the horizontal and vertical centre lines with basting stitches in a light-coloured thread. Set the fabric in a frame or hoop, and count out from the centre to start stitching at a point convenient to you.

One thread of cotton was used in the needle for cross stitches and one for backstitch throughout the design. Work all cross stitches first, making sure that all top stitches run in the same direction. Some quarter stitches are also used in this design; you will find instructions for making these on page 6. Finally, work all backstitch details.

A complete set of alphabets and numerals has been provided to enable you to personalize the pillow. Work out the name and date that you need, using a pencil and graph paper, and then fill it in on the chart itself, making sure that both the name and date are centred on the design.

MAKING THE PILLOW

Gently handwash the finished piece, if necessary, and lightly press with a steam iron on the wrong side. Trim the embroidered fabric to measure 23cm (9¼in) square. Pin the broderie anglaise to the right side of the embroidery, with the decorative edge facing inwards. Trim the ends, if necessary, and join them with a neat french seam.

Gathering it slightly at the corners, baste the broderie anglaise in place, lying just inside the 1cm (⅜in) seam allowance. With right sides together,

pin and stitch the backing fabric and embroidered piece together, leaving a gap of 5cm (2in) at one side.

Clip the corners; turn the cover right side out, and fill with polyester. Slipstitch the opening, and finish by stitching a ribbon bow in each corner of the cushion.

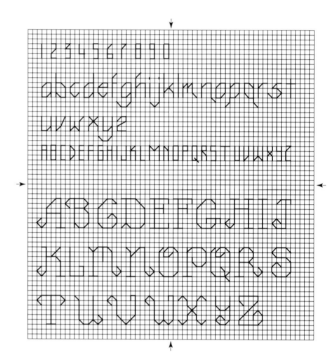

GINGERBREAD COTTAGE ▶			DMC	ANCHOR	MADEIRA
Cross	Half Cross				
X		Pale blue	3752	976	1001
Z	⁄	Soft salmon pink	761	8	0404
+	−	Lilac	554	97	0711
Y	⊔	Soft yellow	744	301	0112
∅		Ecru	Ecru	926	2101
•		White	White	2	White
O		Pale silver grey	762	397	1804
V		Medium straw	3046	373	2103
I		Light straw	3047	886	2205
◪		Medium grey green	522	860	1513
L		Very light grey green	524	858	1511
◇		Apple green	368	261	1310
T		Pale shell pink	3713	23	0608
◢		Medium pink brown	3064	378	2310
∧		Pale pink brown	3773	882	2312
▲		Dark golden brown	610	905	1914
●		Medium golden brown	611	898	2107
■		Medium grey	415	398	1803
N		Medium antique blue	932	920	1710
◔		Medium salmon pink	760	9	0405
	◣	Clear green	3363	262	1311
	⊏	Light grey green	523	859	1512
◻		Very light gold brown	613	831	2109
		Medium steel grey*	646	815	1811

Note: bks all lettering and hearts in medium steel grey (used for bks only), and house and fence in dark golden brown.*

An English Village

This charming picture shows a typical English village scene – a row of small cottages, all of differing styles and periods, nestling together amid the rural setting. It's a timeless scene that is both rewarding to stitch and display with pride in your home.

AN ENGLISH VILLAGE

YOU WILL NEED

For the English Village picture, set in a mount
with a cut-out measuring 17.5cm × 7.5cm
(7in × 3in):

*35cm × 25cm (14in × 10in) of antique white,
14-count Aida fabric*
*Stranded embroidery cotton in the colours given in
the appropriate panel*
No 26 tapestry needle
*Wooden frame, measuring 28cm × 17.5cm
(11¼ × 7in)*
*Rectangular mount, cut to fit the frame, with
cut-out as specified above*
Strong thread and cardboard, for mounting

•

THE EMBROIDERY

Prepare the fabric as described on page 4; find the
centre by folding, and mark the horizontal and
vertical centre lines with basting stitches in a light-
coloured thread. Set the fabric in a frame, and
count out from the centre to start stitching at a point
convenient to you.

Two threads of cotton were used in the needle
for cross stitches and one for backstitch throughout
these designs. Work all cross stitches first, taking
them over one block of fabric and making sure that
all top stitches run in the same direction. Finally,
work all backstitch details.

FINISHING

Gently handwash the finished piece, if necessary,
and lightly press with a steam iron on the wrong
side. Stretch and mount the embroidery as
explained on page 6. Insert it into the frame,
behind the mount. A custom-made frame of dark
wood was used for this picture, to echo the various
shades of brown and gold in the cottage.

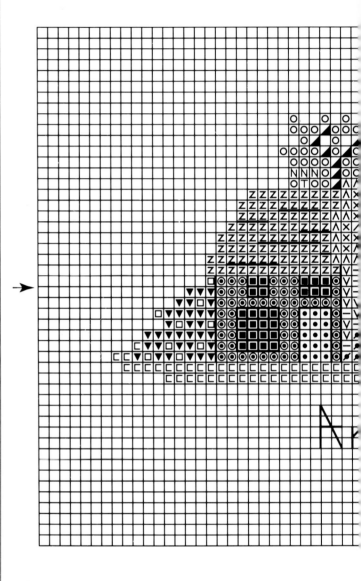

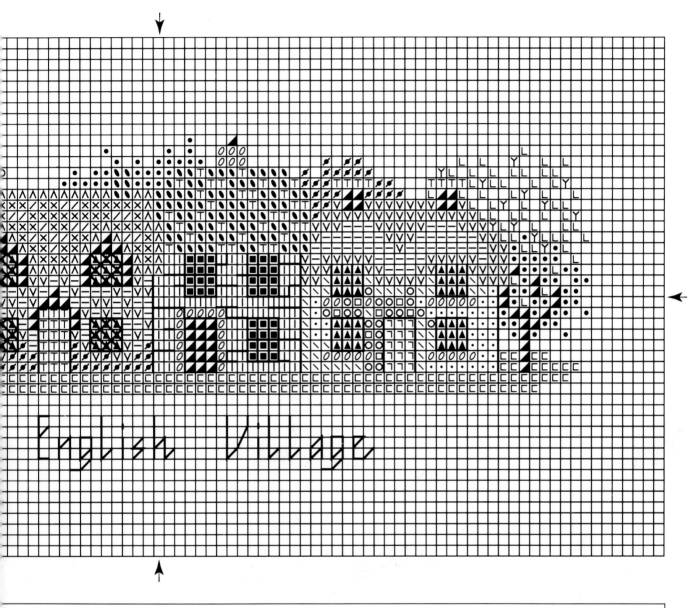

AN ENGLISH VILLAGE ▲

Cross	Half Cross		DMC	ANCHOR	MADEIRA
T		Golden tan	420	375	2104
◪		Medium golden brown	611	889	2107
▲		Dark steel grey	646	815	1811
■		Dull grey	414	400	1801
∧		Dark drab grey	3022	393	1903
✕		Medium steel grey	647	8581	1813
╱		Light steel grey	648	900	1814
◣		Red brown	433	371	2303
⊘		Very light golden brown	613	831	2109
Ⅰ		Very light grey brown	644	830	1907
◪		Light grey green	523	859	1512
V		Medium straw	3047	887	2206
─		Light straw	3046	886	2205
⌐		Soft grey blue	927	849	1708
▢		Light salmon pink	761	8	0404
◎		Light olive green	3053	216	1513

Cross	Half Cross		DMC	ANCHOR	MADEIRA
•		White	White	2	White
◥		Light silver grey	762	397	1804
▼		Apple green	368	261	1310
Y		Yellow	744	301	0112
⦿		Clear green	3363	861	1602
L		Very light grey green	524	858	1511
Z		Dark grey brown	640	903	1905
N		Very dark brown	839	380	1913
		C	Light tan	738	942	2013
◉		Light grey beige	3023	392	1903
		Dark grey*	844	401	1810

Note: bks side walls, doors and lines on left end of roof in very dark brown, window panes in white, window frames in dark grey* (used for bks only), and brickwork on house with rust roof in dark grey brown.

Winter
Cottage

This is a classic winter scene – the
Cotswold cottage of golden stone with
grey thatched roof lies in a fold of the
snow-covered hills. Colour is given to
the winter landscape by the dark
emerald of the evergreens and the
brilliant scarlet of holly berries.
In the foreground, a tree stripped to
winter bareness stands silhouetted
against the pale sky.

WINTER COTTAGE

YOU WILL NEED

For the Winter Cottage picture, set in a mount with a cut-out measuring 16.5cm × 21.5cm (6½in × 8½in):

30cm × 35cm (12in × 14in) of antique white, 14-count Aida fabric
Stranded embroidery cotton in the colours given in the panel
No26 tapestry needle
Wooden frame, measuring 26cm × 30cm (10⅜ × 12in)
Rectangular mount, cut to fit the frame, with cut-out as specified above
Strong thread and cardboard, for mounting

•

THE EMBROIDERY

Prepare the fabric as described on page 4; find the centre by folding, and mark the horizontal and vertical centre lines with basting stitches in a light-coloured thread. Set the fabric in a frame or hoop and count out from the centre to start stitching at a point convenient to you.

Two threads of cotton were used in the needle for cross stitches and one for backstitch *unless* otherwise stated in the colour key. Work all cross stitches first, and then the half crosses, taking them over one block of fabric. Make sure that all top stitches run in the same direction. Finally, work all backstitch details.

FINISHING

Gently handwash the finished piece, if necessary, and lightly press with a steam iron on the wrong side. Finally, stretch and mount the embroidery as explained on page 6. Insert it into the frame, behind the rectangular mount. A subtle wooden frame has been used for all four seasonal cottage pictures, and the colour of the mount has been especially selected in each case to echo colours predominant in the design.

WINTER COTTAGE ▶			DMC	ANCHOR	MADEIRA
Cross	Half Cross				
☒		Golden brown	612	832	2108
◦		Medium golden brown	611	898	2107
Ⓞ		Medium beige grey	642	392	1906
◩		Light beige grey	644	830	1907
▲		Dark olive green	520	269	1514
N		Clear green	3363	262	1311
L		Medium grey green	522	859	1513
⊞		White	White	2	White
	☑	Very pale grey	762	397	1804
	V	Silver grey	415	398	1803
Y		Scarlet	815	43	0513
⊘		Light scarlet	304	47	0509
▣		Very dark grey	844	401	1810
◪		Medium brownish grey	3022	8581	1903
Ⅰ		Light brownish grey	3023	392	1902
◤		Tan	420	375	2104
T		Medium brown gold	372	855	211
∧		Medium straw	3046	887	2206
	Z	Light blue grey	927	849	1708
		Dark brown*	839	360	1914

Note: bks house walls, door, roof, tree trunk, branches and birds with one strand of dark brown (used for bks only), and window panes with two strands of white; when making half stitches with light blue grey, use one strand only.*

ACKNOWLEDGEMENTS

The author would like to thank the following people for their help:

Mike Grey at Framecraft Limited for supplying the various products used for the 'Little Houses' project, and the staff of 'Outlines' Picture Framers, 22 The Pavement, Clapham Common, London SW4, for their friendly and efficient framing of all pictures in this book (with the exception of the Traditional Cottage sampler).

On a personal level, my thanks and gratitude go to my mother and father for all they have given me, and to Terry for his love and support through the endless hours of stitching involved in creating this book.

SUPPLIERS

The following mail order company has supplied some of the basic items needed for making up the projects in this book:

Framecraft Miniatures Limited
372/376 Summer Lane
Hockley
Birmingham, B19 3QA
England
Telephone (021) 359 4442

Addresses for Framecraft stockists worldwide
Ireland Needlecraft Pty Ltd
2-4 Keppel Drive
Hallam, Victoria 3803
Australia

Danish Art Needlework
PO Box 442, Lethbridge
Alberta T1J 3Z1
Canada

Sanyei Imports
PO Box 5, Hashima Shi
Gifu 501-62
Japan

The Embroidery Shop
286 Queen Street
Masterton
New Zealand

Anne Brinkley Designs Inc.
246 Walnut Street
Newton
Mass. 02160
USA

S A Threads and Cottons Ltd.
43 Somerset Road
Cape Town
South Africa

For information on your nearest stockist of embroidery cotton, contact the following:

DMC

UK
DMC Creative World Limited
62 Pullman Road
Wigston
Leicester, LE8 2DY
Telephone: 0533 811040

USA
The DMC Corporation
Port Kearney Bld.
10 South Kearney
N.J. 07032-0650
Telephone: 201 589 0606

AUSTRALIA
DMC Needlecraft Pty
P.O. Box 317
Earlswood 2206
NSW 2204
Telephone: 02599 3088

COATS AND ANCHOR

UK
Kilncraigs Mill
Alloa
Clackmannanshire
Scotland, FK10 1EG
Telephone: 0259 723431

USA
Coats & Clark
P.O. Box 27067
Dept CO1
Greenville
SC 29616
Telephone: 803 234 0103

AUSTRALIA
Coats Patons Crafts
Thistle Street
Launceston
Tasmania 7250
Telephone: 00344 4222

MADEIRA

UK
Madeira Threads (UK) Limited
Thirsk Industrial Park
York Road, Thirsk
N. Yorkshire, YO7 3BX
Telephone: 0845 524880

USA
Madeira Marketing Limited
600 East 9th Street
Michigan City
IN 46360
Telephone: 219 873 1000

AUSTRALIA
Penguin Threads Pty Limited
25-27 Izett Street
Prahran
Victoria 3181
Telephone: 03529 4400